This is Not For You

By Doné de Beer

Copyright © 2025 Doné de Beer

All rights reserved. No part of this book may be used or reproduced in any form without the prior written permission of the author, except in the context of reviews or academic purposes.

ISBN: 978-1-7640163-0-8

First edition: 2025.

Published by Doné de Beer.

Melbourne, Australia.

This is a work of creative nonfiction. While inspired by real events, certain details have been changed for artistic and privacy reasons. Any resemblance to actual persons, living or dead, is purely coincidental.

This book deals with themes of trauma, abuse and toxic relationships. Reader discretion is advised.

Cover design by George Miroshnichenko.

Printed by Ingram Spark.

Some poems in this collection first appeared in the following publications:

Shhh and Is it Really Abuse if You Were Never Hit? – Empyrean Magazine

The Blue Mountains – Catchment Literary Journal

Transmutation – Pink Panther Magazine

For the past version of myself who left, even though it was the hardest thing to do.

Table of Contents

Part I : The Breaking

A Guidebook : Please Read Instructions

Satellite

Red Is the Colour Of…

No One's Safe

Hungry For What I Am

The Strongest Link / The Weakest Chain

A Role to Play

Bloublasie

shhhh

The Universe

Is it Really Abuse if You Were Never Hit?

Halloween Year One

Transmutation

The Infection: Part One

Swallowing My Sense of Self Bit by Bit

A Guidebook : Please Ignore

Part II : The Healing

We Collapsed

So, I left

Erased

The Blue Mountains

In Which We Run into Each Other, and it Doesn't Mean a Thing

Who the Fuck Am I to You?

Willow Tree

Halloween Year Two

I Don't Know How to Fix This

Can We Meet Again For the First Time?

Betrayal

The Infection: Part Two

The Structure of a Spine

The First Thing I Did For Myself

You Can't Take This

Healing is Never Easy, but it is Always Necessary

To the One Who Comes Next

Over a Year Gone

Part One:
The Breaking

A Guidebook: Please Read Instructions

When there is a live wire circled around your achilles,
you go to stand your ground
and find it's easier to give way.
So you do.
Over and over and over and
(you had nothing to apologise for in the first place.)
Know that this is your sign to leave.

When that clear line between reality and falsehoods
starts to teeter.
Your bare feet pressed against the white dotted lines
that keeps shifting positions.
(you know your version of facts was right, yeah?)
Know that this is your sign to leave.

When you can't look your friends in the eyes anymore.
Because it feels too much
like confession,
like admitting something you're not willing to.
The excuses you give to yourself
don't hold up in the light of their worried gaze.

(would you want them to stay with a partner like yours?)
Know that this is your sign to leave.

When the sound of your ringtone scares you so much
you put your phone on silent for months.
Still flinching at the sight of a missed call
because you know there will be a price to pay.
(you should never be afraid of the one you love.)
Know that this is your sign to leave.

When he says
But I've never hit you before.
Like that's some kind of accomplishment.
Like that's something you should be grateful for.
(it doesn't have to be physical to count as abuse.)
Know that this is your sign to leave.

When lying next to him feels like a jailor's sentence.
Where the crime keeps changing
on his every whim.
(there's a reason you don't want him to touch you anymore.)
Know that this is your sign to leave.

When he is sweet to you and all you can think is
for how long?

When the crying comes more than the laughing.

When the gifts feel like bribes.

When you start to question your own reality.

When you stop writing. WHEN YOU STOP WRITING.

When caring about anything feels like too much effort.

When fighting for yourself is too tiring.

When you are drowning in the pain of his sadness.

When you are floating in the ecstasy of his kindness.

And especially when you are clinging
so *viciously* **desperately** to him.

Because you are so so in love.

please leave him please **please**

Satellite

1 missed call

2 missed calls

3 missed calls

4 missed calls

5 missed calls

6 missed calls

7 missed calls

8 missed calls

9 missed calls

10 missed calls

11 missed calls

- This is how love turns into fear.

Please just give me some space

Red is the colour of...

Rage

was never far from you.

Always lying in the chasm between

your eye teeth and incisors.

I tried to find ways to walk with a lighter footstep.

But still, I find myself stumbling upon it,

stretched out beneath your toes,

snubbed

and spoiling for a fight.

My nerves have been replaced with piano wire,

sharpened, but much, much thinner.

There is a certain music to this kind of pain.

Everything was an invitation for your anger.

Maybe I should've learned

quicker what action not to take

what words not to say, and especially

in what particular way.

Your sadness is a gaping mouth, hungry and wet.

This is rock bottom, this is the lowest I've ever been.

But so was last week, and the week before,

and the week before.

Of course you can interrogate me on my whereabouts from Saturday night, six months ago, why am I looking at you bleary-eyed and confused, why am I not answering your questions, yes, its 1am but

Where was I that Saturday?

You adore that particular shhkk sound a backbone makes when it snaps under your demands.

How you become enraptured with breaking, and I, with being broken

It's addictive – having everyone on my side.

I give in to you over and over and

try on different platitudes -

I could be the pleading damsel or the apologetic sinner.

The scathing bitch or the weeping woman.

The girl in love or the girl you'll leave.

They are all true in some version of your mind.

They are all real in some version of myself.

Somewhere inside me something is burning.

How I offer myself up to you again and again and again.

No One's Safe

I hate how I was just the perfect victim for you.

They say the narcissists don't go for the quiet shy ones.

Oh no,

they go for the loud ones with a bleeding heart and something to prove.

How I passed every test of yours

so exceedingly well, so eagerly,

endlessly starved for your approval.

The deer begs for the headlights.

I had my ultimatums,

like they could protect me from love's worst bite.

If he ever hits me…

I'm leaving immediately.

But what if he never hits you?

What if that isn't the worst thing he could do to you?

I thought I was too smart

to ever fall for a ploy like this.

The one where the boy pours all of his love into the girl

and then thimble by thimble

starts to extract it from her.

Needle sharp,

your dismissal is a pain as

damaging as a missed heartbeat.

It is terrifying,

the things you will tolerate

when you are warmed to it degree by degree.

Do you think the frogs knew

of their impending demise

and chose to stay anyways?

Hungry For What I Am

I was a starving child.
Overfed on stories, I find words dissipate
as soon as the last page is turned.
Fey food revealed to be rotting carcasses, magots.
Restore the enchantment! I demand.
I begin, once again, to gorge myself.
I was not a patient child.

I was a ravenous teenager.
Devouring these books like it could deliver me
a hero's arc, my own world full of people to save,
and I, the only one who can do so.
(maybe being the Chosen One will finally heal my wound of
not feeling wanted.)
How I tried to play saviour for friend after friend after friend.
I was not a peaceful teenager.

I was an insatiable adult.
The time for reveals and letters and quests had come
and gone.
Now I had only myself to feed upon.

Now I am tape worm to my own intestines, magots and a rotting carcass.

Until you came.

So,

Serpentine vulture - pick at the remains of me.

There is a story here, you just don't know it yet.

Lay out a buffet for me, sugared words and candied promises.

Spin me on the pinpoint of your lies, wrap me up so sweet.

You prince-villain, find me another world.

I will let you digest me bit by bit.

You are a venomous adult.

Seeking platitudes, pandering, and

constant pacifying.

Your ego finds everything to be a pain point.

How closely you protect the idea that it is the

World at fault. Not you.

A generational curse.

From your father's father to your father to you.

There is nothing that will make it okay what happened to you.

There is nothing that will excuse what you did to me.

The Strongest Link / The Weakest Chain

I will never heal from you.

You will always be here.

Puppet strings laced through my hair,

I go to speak and

find the words that leave

my mouth are not mine,

but yours.

Am I becoming to others

what you were to me?

Needy, demanding.

A neurotic mess, an exhausting burden.

Am I hurting the people around me

with my own grief?

It is a cruel thing to be so aware of it

but helpless to change it.

I will never be okay and there is nothing,

nothing I can do about it.

There is no soft love for me, no forever.

If I want to be adored, then I must take the abuse with it.

But I wanted to be worshipped –

Didn't I?

To be viewed as something divine,

mystical.

Something beyond your human imperfection.

In your eyes I can be placed higher than I ever was.

(I am so failingly human.)

Well, ruling a boy's heart takes sacrifice.

And if it is all of my joy I must surrender,

then maybe that is okay

for just

a splinter

of a

moment

where I

finally

get to

be

somebody's

number

one.

I have been wrong before.

I can be wrong about this too.

A Role To Play

You are a pretend god of dreams
and I am a girl without religion.
Let me bow down and confess all my mistakes to you.
Each and every one of them.

My accountability like a magic eraser board handed to you.
We can erase both our sins at once if we just slide
the panel right.
No, let's not compare scribbles.
We've both made a mess of things so who cares
which side is darker.
I am very lucky you are choosing to wipe this all clean.

The pulley system of   my nerves

and your moods

                         up
When you are
I am released.

When you are

                        down

I am strung taut.

By now I should be better at tracking your movements.
I shouldn't be yanked like this every time.
I shouldn't be crying like your cruelty is something new.

Was the pedestal you put me on too high?
Was the fall from it too painful to watch?
When you're so used to stacking the corpses of
past relationships to elevate yourself,
could you ever see me as anything other than a
stepladder for your reputation as someone
wronged by the world?

When an abuser is unable to control you anymore
they will manipulate how others view you.
You will try and turn everyone against me.

It's your word against my word against your word

against my word against your word

and you are so skilled at changing the narrative.

When they were your friends first, did I ever

really stand a chance?

Even though you were the one lying

YOU WERE THE ONE LYING.

You had this particular talent of

admitting wrongdoing without taking any actual responsibility.

And I fell for it each time.

So desperate to just be okay again,

I didn't care what price I had to pay to bring back

the strawberry moon and laughter.

Bloublasie

Blue bottle tail

strung around my legs.

Stinging clinginess.

Sharp and sudden.

I try and peel it off but

everywhere I touch burns burns burns.

Invisible nettle, scorch

and settle,

for this crisis controlled.

I see everyone else is crying too,

so I suck back my tears and act

like the pain isn't so

painful after all.

Picking grime out from under my nails of

another night spent

digging up the hatchet.

There are some fights that are too ridiculous

to form a defence against.

I try to peel you off me but

my hands blister and burn burn burn.

Read me the palm lines of these white-red scars.

Spell out my future or trace me back through my past.

How many times will my inner child be

dragged through the mud?

She has to know I'm doing this all for her.

Is this not what she wanted?

To be loved to be loved to be loved.

shhhh

i tremble into existence / paint white lies red / adopt whatever
personality you've given me today

befriend these little demons of mine / it's playtime

if i cannot endure my own loneliness

then at least let me ease another's

you are moth born / i am the flame at fault

this waning is not natural \ we are not a blood moon

i do not revel at all this red \ i don't take lightly to how
you are draining me

torn ligaments of a question mark / i lie / shallow breaths

i'm doing everything they say you should \ but all i hear is static

we are a makeshift grenade / in a stick shift car \ i never
learnt how to drive

we are not in orbit \ we are not being held
together by circling one another

we are a collision that has / already happened / is
happening / will happen

call it what you want but i haven't felt a thing for weeks

crevassing into splinters of the mind / this pain is
so wide \ but this crack is so narrow

i go blue for days / quiver at the sight of red and

try to abandon my anger \ only to find it is still

there where i left it \

i am one of those cavers / that have wandered too far off path

when does exploration turn into survival

when does curiosity turn into casualties

how much can i endure of your loneliness

before i am merged with you

at what point can i stop calling this okay / and start calling it

abuse

i would

/ take a pickaxe to the wall of this mine / to what is mine /

\ even if it collapses / even if i collapse inside it \

/ i can quit any day now / i can leave anytime i want /

/ i can quit any day now \

/

/

/

/

how does the body live on after the heart has died

how do i learn to stop loving someone

The Universe

I know I shouldn't, but sometimes –
I look back with distaste at the girl I was,
when I was with you.
The neuroticizes, the fairy wearing boots, the girl
in your dreams.
So desperately ready to *save you*.

They say your intuition has three ways of
telling you when something is wrong –

First, it's a feather –

Whisper of an itch.
That spot on your back
just out of reach.
You know the one.
To the right of your shoulder blade,
that dip just before your jutting spine.
You can feel it now, can't you?
You roll your shoulders, twist this way and that,
try to ignore it.

Next is a brick –

Through the window of your glass-pane beliefs.

The hypnotic jerk out of a microsleep.

(you know people can die on the roads from that yeah?)

This heightened awareness,

grip tight on the wheel,

eyes wary on him,

that lurching heartbeat of static,

doesn't last very long.

It's not much further to go, you reason.

Just a little bit longer.

Soon your awareness dissipates,

runs its fingers over the road,

the trees flicking by,

how good things are going to be again,

his promises.

Your eyelids start to flicker.

You can't seem to fight against its downwards pull.

Millimetre by millimetre,

you go on autopilot, accepting his abuse becomes

an automatic process.

Then it's a bus –

Your ribcage is the first point of contact.
If we were to slow this disaster down enough.
(you know how easy it is to miss things in the heat of the fight.)
You can hear the way it cracks inwards
millimetre by millimetre,
before simply shattering into splinters.
You fold forwards, a kiss to the temple.
Collision to mutilation in a matter of moments.
The first drop of blood has barely fallen and
you are already unrecognisable.

Now let's say you come out of it unscathed.
It was just a love tap after all.
Wouldn't you get up?
Wouldn't you look both ways?
If you see the bus coming and still step out on the road,
is it really the driver's fault when your ribcage caves in?
Can you even remember who you are when you've
stayed,
and stayed,
and stayed?

What if I was the bus driver.

What if I was the passengers and the girl getting hit.

I was the road and the green light that turned orange just a second too late.

I was the faulty brake and the tires worn down to nothing.

I was every piece and splinter of this destruction.

So what comes after the bus then?

Another one

                              And another one

                                                    And another one

I think the universe is starting to revel in teaching me my lesson.

Is it Really Abuse if You Were Never Hit?

I want to be struck to sicken and rot.

To have something black and blue to point to

when the people ask:

What happened to you?

What did he do to you?

Words do not break bones, actually.

Words do not leave any traces at all, really.

Circumstantial evidence, they'll say.

It's all conjecture, he'll reason.

He said I'll never find a love like this again.

- *I sure fucking hope not*

Halloween - Year One

Still my favourite holiday. Even now.

Did you know how worried I was that you would ruin it?

But of course,

I told you *don't ask me to be your girlfriend on Halloween.*
Any day but that.
I'm ready to say yes. Just -
please don't make our anniversary on Halloween.

But you did it anyways.

Funny,

how you were crossing boundaries and ignoring

my wishes from the start.

How I thought it was so romantic.

The night of –

Halloween is here.

You pick me up late but don't tell me where we're going.

When I see the sand dunes, I mistake them for snow.

The brain is funny like that.

They are the colour of scraped bone and bleached sawdust.

The ocean is so much louder at night.

Sticky and swollen,

the blood moon is more of a hazy orange.
Earlier, I carved a pumpkin with you for the first time.
It rots within days.

Halloween –
The almost-storm heat of it, the grey-purple clouds so sullen.
The way there never really was a true spring in Melbourne just wintersummer smashed together.
Splintered with the coldest of rains
back to back with a heat haze.
The fine line between the shaking rains and
the placid blue skies
draws closer and closer.
We put cinnamon and maple syrup on everything.
Watch horror movie after horror movie.
How my brain gets tired of fight or flight simulations,
and decides to just stay.

The moon promised blood and so you had it.

Transmutation

Funny how girl can become graveyard.

How you make her cemetery of your pain.

Bouquets of flowers,

headstones marked with names upon names upon names

that are not hers.

How she carries the weight of all your failed relationships,

from your ex-girlfriend

to your father.

The boy is a magician.

He pulls rabbits out of hats,

halves people,

vanishes blame

and makes it reappear on the girl's shoulders.

The girl is lighthouse.

She is supposed to guide him home.

Weather his storms, shine light

each day every day each day every day.

He dashes upon rocks when she is not there,

doesn't she know that? Doesn't she care?

The boy is matchstick wrists.

The boy is gasoline veins.

The boy is quick flick cigarette lies

and the archer bow's shape

of a mouth

when he says I do nothing but cry

and I cry and I cry.

The girl is a lie is a lie is a lie.

The boy is sinking ship.

The boy is ocean in storm.

The boy just wants home.

Can the girl not see this?

Does the girl not care?

The Infection: Part One

Stage I : Contamination

You don't know this yet

But the infection is here

Taking over

Multiplying

It is already in your cells

Stage II : Diagnosis

There are days

Slipping away

His mouth is opening wider

I'm being swallowed and

I've never seen what a person

looks like from the inside

Swallowing My Sense of Self Bit by Bit

And I let the boy kiss me,

even though I want to pull my teeth out and

swallow them whole.

Just so I can gnaw upon his sadness.

They do not cut on the way down.

Throat slime contract,

retract, how easy it slips

down.

Itch of intestine.

Digest the feeling. Intellectualised and parsed out.

Acidic decompose,

spew pewter and powdered bone.

There is something monstrous bubbling up inside of me.

Swallow it down swallow it down.

Develop an appetite for pain.

I turn blue as it crawls back to me.

Sick distaste I'll spit you out I'll spit you out.

Phagocyte frenzy engulf everything EVERYTHING.

Even what is mine.

When are there enough foreign cells

for me to no longer be me?

Perhaps I am evidence that wanting love is a sickness.

Become nutrition, nexus of disease.

Packageable consumption.

I am water to his thirst, then I turn to

solar flare sun burst.

How he adores me when I shine.

Tongue on the copper wire he strips back slowly,

so slowly, what made him soft.

What made him safe.

Flicker flicker.

Insist it will be like it used to be. It will be! It will be!

Prodded by my dogtooth I stutter on tangible reasons.

Internal bleeding, I am rotting on nostalgia,

white spores mould-fluff upon which I heap

promises promises.

Blood ooze and thicken, tremble.

I'll gut you I'll string you up by your tongue if you say

one more time you're going to change and then
just stay the same.
Salivating at the possibility of release.
There are rabid dogs and then there is me.

I am starting to realise that you, fire, you
are growing with every one of my exhales.
You are oxygen starved, and I am haemoglobin.
Blood thinning to water so that you
can be the strongest bond.

Metastasising, minor hurts become cancerous.
I am proving something here, can't you see
I am gritting my, well…

My mouth yawns open.
Pink sludge of gums slime slicked,
glistening wetly.
There is such revulsion in absence.
Such a terror in being separated.
So what if I will never trust myself again?
I have teeth in my stomach
and they want to devour everything.

A Guidebook : Please Ignore

So you wanna know why I stayed, huh?

You want to know what, reasonably rational, person

would go through all that pain for

months and months and months

(which I've so nicely condensed to the last 35 pages for you)

And. Still. Not. Leave.

Well, here it is then.

Once upon a time

there was a girl and there was a boy

and they were in love.

This was the girl's first love, and you know

what they say about first loves.

I will never forget you.

I didn't have to ask him to buy me flowers, you know?

He just did. And not just once, but again and again.

We would go to gigs together and he would put me up

on his shoulders, so that I can actually see

all our favourite bands.

We introduced new music to one another and created playlists just for each other.

Road trips and extravagant dates planned.

Always, always some kind of adventure.

That family holiday he came on,
the synergy of giddiness that
stretched in the space between us.

And laughter, oh, so much laughter.

There barely went by an hour where I wasn't
head tipped back eyes screwed shut from laughing so hard.

You felt familiar to me from the moment we met, there was something of fate in it, something of inevitability.

You made space for my silliness and my sadness.

You held me in the way I needed to be
and wanted to know everything about me.

Always remembering those little details.

How I like my tea, my biggest regrets, my favourite food, the things I adored and the things I hated.

I got to know him too.

All those little details.

How he liked his tea, his biggest regrets, his favourite food, the things he adored (me) and the things he hated (me).

It is a beautiful and sacred thing to watch someone unfold.

To peer into every part and brush your fingertips over it.
He was warm, silly, adventurous, clever, creative, prone to melodrama but always entertaining, funny, insightful and I was utterly and completely in love with him.

Those first eleven months were blissful.
If we had ended there, it's likely you would've gone down as one of the great loves of my life.
Then again, maybe not.
There were signs even then, but what's a few concerns in the face of overwhelming infatuation,
spurned by the ricochet of love bombing.

How I let you abuse me for months just to
      taste a sliver
           of a sliver
                of a sliver
of that happiness again.

I think people need to stop asking

Why do women stay?

And instead start asking

Why do men harm?

Part Two:
The Healing

we collapsed.

black hole

sucking everything

everything in

twin bushfires

one set alight to

erase the other

or just two people

who didn't work

together anymore

So, I Left

The sky an unblinking eye.

Lungs deflating, head tilted back

a single breath   out.

At first, it is only lightness.

I fall asleep easily that night.

And the next and the next and the next.

At first it is celebrations.

Friends that are proud, so so proud of me.

How strong I am,

how brave,

how happy they are

now that it's all finally over.

But then,

Recovery tips towards despair,

the phoenix paradox:

are you the flames I rise from

or the fire bird that won't stop climbing out of my ashes?

Waking hours are the clipping of a

fingernail between

my third and fourth vertebrae.

Move on too quickly and

this tightrope begins to wobble.

Move on too slowly and

it starts to shake, momentum lost,

I teeter.

When you have lived in this wound for so long

it does not feel like recovery to leave.

Don't you know not to pull the knife out?

It was so much easier to just be in pain.

You're still the only person I have loved.

Even now, three years on.

You're still the only person that has come closest to

destroying me.

~~erased~~

I want to live in a world where you do not exist.
Where I don't flinch at my ringtone,
I don't shrink in the face of new love.
I am bold and vulnerable, lying belly side up to the world,
and I am not afraid of showing
my softest parts.

I want to live in a world where your name
has never been spoken.
Where I don't second,
and third, and fourth guess my every word,
I don't assign blame like target practice, red marker
circling my own head shot.
I am vibrant and steady, loving myself in a way that doesn't
shake at the thought of someone not liking me.
My boundaries are firm, and I do not apologise for the things
I am not sorry for.

I want to live in a world where you have never touched me.
Where I don't turn my body into graveyard | lighthouse.
My kindness nailed to the moth wings of good intentions.

I am calm and at ease,

my mind is a haven of serenity.

My thoughts are softly crashing ocean waves

lulling me too sweet,

sweet rest.

I want to live in a world where I am free of your

trauma dogging my every step.

Free of your nails in the ridges of ribcage,

free of your bleeding heart

stuffed down my throat, choking, choking.

You are not here you are not here

you are not here you are not here.

I want to live in a world where you do not exist,

and I am finally free.

The Blue Mountains

In the crevice of my boot soles still lies dirt
from the Blue Mountains we trekked last winter. I keep
finding traces of you, even when I've scrubbed the wound
raw.

I can still taste the crunchy-softness of homemade bread
and the sweet-spice of pumpkin soup at the Yellow Deli.
I still recall your kindness-cruelty.
How so many things exist in contradiction.

I dream of getting in my car and driving the
same roads we did. Retracing the dips and
bends, the stretches of dry fields –
broken up by scraps of new growth.
Feverishly green.

Just a few months ago a fire
razed this whole country to the ground.
Just a few months ago we were
perfectly fine (I swear).
I would mimic the way we played the music

loud enough to feel it in our teeth.

Windows all the way down, I can't hear the words.

You are driving so fast.

I would follow the M1 too, I'd stick my

head out the window,

my hair movie-wild,

sun-drenched,

feverishly alive,

scream-sing along with the music,

let myself laugh again.

My car would give out before I even reached the border.

In Which We Run Into Each Other, and It Doesn't Mean a Thing

I can say with absolute certainty that I have thought through
every possible scenario in which we meet.
I have cast us in different roles for each one,
built a new setting,
re-worked the lines.

I think I can say with absolute certainty
that I am ready if we do meet.
I have my quips, I know where to pause dramatically,
where to lean back with a raised eyebrow.
Yes, you could go off script but your
rage-pleading, your cruel-kindness
has become very familiar to me.
There is a finite number of combinations to this dance.
You might step sideways,
but I am no longer on the back foot.

In all of these scenarios I can never see myself as anything
other than on top (at last).

Who the Fuck Am I to You?

If my identity was defined by your opinion of me

then I would've finally achieved

all my childhood dreams

of becoming a shapeshifter.

Want to hear me repeat the age-old line

careful what you wish for?

I start out as the kind loving girlfriend,

but by the end of act two

I'm a cruel heartless bitch.

From liar to sweetheart, terrible to beautiful,

the object of your adoration to the thing

you'll inevitably discard.

And then back again.

And back again.

The strongest woman you've ever met,

to a pathetic girl that won't stop crying.

The person who has done the most for you anyone ever has,

to the girl who has never been there for you.

These changes come more swiftly.

I'm starting to forget my original form.

How can I exist in such multitudes within your mind?

Which one is real?

To the wolf, the human is the other form.

To the human, the wolf is the other form.

I stopped caring which one is true,

I stopped looking at the phases of the moon.

I don't want to be anything at all to you.

Willow Tree

You told me

you would

wait for me

under a

willow tree

if you were

to ever

die before

me

so I burned

every

willow tree

to the ground

I do not want

to meet you

again

in this life

or the next

Halloween - Year 2

Our first (and only) anniversary –

It isn't even daybreak yet and we are

already fighting.

Anger from last night spills over,

I keep my worst words between my eye teeth and incisors but

somehow you still find them.

I'm crying.

Again.

You're lying.

Most likely.

We find some sliver of peace by dinner.

Get into our costumes –

A girl who won't sign her name away

and a boy whose only half alive.

How ironic.

We haven't had sex in a while.

I don't want you touching me.

A year after –

What once marked our anniversary,

now means nothing.

How I longed for the girl I used to be.

How I now revel in the fact that she's dead.

The before-you during-you version of me was:

Carefree, naïve, kind – sometimes at her own expense, very trusting, always nervous, neurotic even, prone to picking out the best in people no matter how deeply it's buried.

Well,

Some things need to be sacrificed.

It is Halloween after all.

Some things need to stay dead.

(you murdered that girl, and I buried her.)

I Don't Know How to Fix This

i'm sorry that i'm too much.

that i say yes when asked *you okay?* ... no, i'm not. i'm sorry that i have no emotional permeance, so i keep asking do you still like me do you still like me do you still like me do you still like me. a neurotic mess. i orbit my self-worth around your opinion of me don't you know the earth is not the centre of the universe. i am not the centre of myself. i do this with everyone i've ever met. even that lady on the train can't you see. she knows each dark movement of my heart each pathetic way i plead for something better. than this.

i'm sorry that i haven't healed from my trauma yet.
i say that i'll do better but i just do the same. slipping back into bad habits, these habits are so bad, i know, i know. i will unlearn them, just give me some time. and more. and more. i just need some more time. can't you spare a little bit of fucking patience. mercy. forgiveness. can't you be who i was to him? healer and sanctimonious forgiver. everything must come back to my abusive ex. if not then what was it all for, all of me for, i always make it all about me. i'm sorry. i have not practiced active listening or follow up questions. i have not practiced

unravelling my victim complex, even if maybe, yes, this one time i was, in fact, a victim. i'm sorry for the space i have sequestered and claimed for myself, if i could give it away. minimize it. maybe briefly misplace it – i would. i could come back to it in four years when the blood wound is white scar (they told me to just give it time. i have been counting the days until it's been 'enough time'.)

i'm sorry i don't know how to care without getting completely attached. so now that's your problem to deal with. by falling madly in love with me right this second. but NOT love bombing me no that would be toxic that would be bad (but maybe just a little wouldn't hurt). i'm sorry that i spiral every time i think you're upset with me, wondering. do you still like me do you still like me do you still like me. i'm sorry that i need constant reassurance and that nothing you say seems too actually work or make me feel better but also don't stop.

i'm sorry for blaming myself for absolutely everything that goes wrong. like how can one person be responsible for literally EVERYTHING that goes wrong. what can i say. i'm a miracle worker. no other abuse survivor has had a warped sense of self and blame. this disease should be named after me.

i am the one who discovered it after all.

i'm sorry that i keep comparing you to everyone who has ever hurt me. even that kid in kindergarten who destroyed my sandcastle cause that really hurt you know. that took a really long time to build. i am taking so much more time rebuilding myself. i'm sorry for hurting you and i'm sorry for hurting me. but maybe it's okay, we're both trying our best, and we are only failingly human after all, of course we're going to make mistakes. everyone deserves grace and understanding. other than my psychotic ex – no he RUINED my life. HE – shit. sorry. i made it about my ex again. okay let's try this again. no really. let's try THIS again.

i've been doing the shadow work the inner child work the healing work the therapy work the work work but. nothing. is. fucking. working. i'm sorry that i keep dismissing my own feelings. i'm sorry for not handling all of this better. i'm sorry that i keep saying sorry to you and. not myself. i'm sorry for being a burden. i'm sorry i don't love myself enough to want better. than this. and most of all. i'm sorry that there aren't enough sorrys in the world to fix me.

I have nothing to apologise for the ways
I have broken during the healing.

Can We Meet Again For the First Time?

I wish I had met you when I was healed.
I promise I wasn't always jagged angles,
such sharp edges. I used to be soft, and sweet,
and didn't wield my bitterness like it was the punch line of a
joke but no one is laughing.

I wish I could erase the trauma he gave to me.
Siphon it off oil trade. Excavate a thousand years of pain.
I'm not the first woman to go through this.
I could make money off of this.
Cart away barrels and barrels of it.
Maybe I should just focus on being happy.

I'm not asking you to heal me.
(I swear.)
I have to do that on my own.
What I would like to ask is –
Could you be something solid I put my back up against
as I do so?
…
But, well, I don't trust you enough to turn around.

So here we are, at standstill, and I won't be the first to lower my guard.

Please.

CAN'T YOU JUST GO FIRST??

I loved myself for one year and I don't know if
I'll ever be able to again.

My mind is a pitfall of sharpened teeth, and I am one wrong move away from falling in.

I am one heartbreak away from jumping.

I AM TIRED!!

This awaiting of the next disaster.

This constant back and forth.

Why wait to stroke the ego again with

I KNEW IT I FUCKING KNEW IT.

Self-confirmed bias or actually a decent intuition?

I ration out my affections, gauge how far you've gone and always draw short of it.

So, if this does break down, I can rest assured knowing *you cared much more than I ever did.*

(I swear.)

And I know *IT'S FUCKED UP.*

I promise I wasn't always tooth-trap.

Salivating at the prospect of new love,

but snapping shut when it actually draws close.

I don't enjoy the taste of your blood, I don't enjoy watching you suffer like this.

I really really don't want you to leave.

I used to let anyone in,

hinge pin heart,

perhaps more people pleaser than genuine compassion.

Yes, of course people still left.

Yes, of course it still hurt.

But this incisor trap has turned inwards.

There is a two-beat mechanical sound to a person taking their first step away from you.

A cocking of some kind of weapon.

You just have to listen closely enough to hear it.

It is never them who is hurt upon the leaving.

It's always me. It's always me.

At least I have something to attribute it all towards.

Can I blame all my failings upon him? (no)

YOU HAVE NO IDEA WHAT HE DID TO ME WHAT HE PUT ME THROUGH.

I **want** to tell you about him, I **want** to hear you say

I'm sorry, I'm so sorry you went through that.

I would never do that to you.

(you swear?)

How do I hide the damage?

How do I secret away this cold neurosis that grows by the day, counting out each way you've already grown uninterested in me.

The messages left on seen, the sudden coldness, the flimsy excuses.

How do I hide this bleeding heart that clings to my sleeve like a distraught child.

Begging to look, hey look at me, hey look, hey look

JUST FUCKING SEE ME

please.

Just see me for the girl I used to be.

She had to be here somewhere still (I swear).

But really, I don't need anyone else.

I don't need you.

I swear.

But fuck,

It would be nice to have you in my corner.

Betrayal

I was so so so angry at you for such a long time.

The abuse, the manipulation, the lies,

the disrespect, the gaslighting.

But when the flame dimmed,

I found anger for myself, too.

For putting up with your treatment.

For all the times I gave in and compromised.

(Not once did I stand my ground, not

once did I have my own back).

For all the apologies I gave when I did nothing wrong.

For all the ways I betrayed myself so that you felt okay.

For all the moments I shrunk myself so you could be on top.

What you did broke me.

But what hurts worse is

I let you.

The Infection: Part Two

Stage III : Treatment

Your friend's words start too finally

catch up to you.

You didn't want to

hear them before.

But you hear them now.

Stage IV : Recovery

When they tell you the virus is gone,

believe them.

The Structure of a Spine

I tried to be happy, but I forgot the shape of my
Spine
of a book balanced in your palm.
Read to me again – the story of how this went.
Am I the shadows on the wall or the torch giving you
Light
of the day makes all these fights look so silly,
am I not being so silly right now?

A bushfire at the door and I am too infatuated with
Annihilation
is my favourite movie, but you already knew that, didn't you?
If cancer is yourself turned foreign, then at
some point we mutated.
How else could we go from love to abuse in a
matter of months?
(maybe it was there all along).
Is there a pride to be found in
those who stay after the evacuation
Calls
upon missed calls upon missed calls upon missed calls.

But it's my fault I picked up the phone.
You are the earthquake, but somehow, I am the
fault line shifting.
I am always at fault, right?
I've been walking on a live wire strung through my stomach
and you never even asked if I'd like to come
Down
this rabbit-curious girl falls and falls and falls and
don't you just love seeing me falter from such a great height?

A queen no longer, just a girl you can
Manipulate
this tale again, you do it so well.
But this is my home, they all say.
But this is my home, I say.

Homes can change.
Girls can rip their own hearts out and eat it bloody and raw.
What I mean to say is : I left I left I left I left I left, and
I am not going
Back
bone so steady now.

The First Thing I Did for Myself

I have not once been sorry
for ending things the way I did.

I relish the pain it caused you.
I hope to God it fucking hurt.

You Can't Take This

For the first time, in a very long time,

I feel like myself again.

As if

all the bones and muscles and sinew of my being

are no longer pulled taught,

but placed in perfect alignment, co-existing peacefully.

They are no longer seeking ways to

grow smaller and smaller until they are but

thimble sized.

You are not in my life anymore.

You are not in my life anymore and I am breathing

deeply, steadily.

You tried so hard, didn't you?

To steal my kindness, wear it like a second skin.

Of course you were jealous of me, of my life.

I didn't live it by the dictations of others.

I wasn't afraid to be seen at the bottom, climbing my way up.

My happiness was something steady, present like the moon

and sure, sometimes it waned.

But I knew it was there.

Your joy was something like the change of seasons.

No matter how many years you lived,

you remained unconvinced every winter that the

sun will ever get warmer, the days will get longer.

That spring will ever come.

You continually needed proof, always convinced

that the next frost will be forever.

You were so desperate to feel alive again.

You so badly wanted to be happy

in a way that didn't disappear by the next breath.

You are not in my life anymore and I have so much free time.

I fill it with all of my favourite things.

Movie nights with my family and day trips to Mt Dandenong,

books devoured in one sitting, days by the beach and nights

spent dancing, hours of laughter and conversation with friends.

I try new things too.

New uni classes, new outfits, I try my eyeliner in different ways,

pole dancing, white water rafting, the gym for the first time,

lookouts you've never seen, I go to gigs by myself, I kiss new

people, I take myself out on dates.

I fall in love all over again – with myself.

It is the most beautiful love story of all.

Healing is Never Easy, But it is Always Necessary

It is a beautiful thing to be growing.

To step back into this body,

mind wary hands shaky, but that's okay.

I have dug trenches within myself.

Burrows and holes to fall down and down and down.

Fill them up fill them up fill them up.

I am –

That spill of sunlight through the clouds.

Gentle and golden and faces turning towards me.

That ferocious forever-changing ocean.

(there is so much still to be discovered).

That moment after the first particle collision all –

I am here I am here I am here!

There was nothing before and now | suddenly |

Oh, how there is eruption and noise and creation

and so much, there is so much here

(to be grateful for).

I am not –

Yours.

Another notch for your beliefs of a world

that has wronged you or

a hinge pin in the dam of your abandonment issues,

or a body to supress your clamouring fears that everyone

leaves you.

I am not a graveyard, I am not a girl cut in half.

I am not a headstone to be marked with name upon

name upon name.

I am so proud of the depths I have plunged to.

The lengths I have traversed.

The heights I have soared to.

Growing growing growing.

But there is much, much further to go still.

(but it's okay if you would just like to rest here for a while).

To the One Who Comes Next
(warning: contents fragile)

know i have been hurt before. badly. love has been train wrecks and car crashes and every cliché of destruction. you could be an original pain or the one to treat me right. it could start with me. yes, you could say i was head over heels in love. much in the way jack was head over heels before he cracked his skull open.

i suffer from a shrinking problem, boys open their mouths and suddenly i am a two feet tall pixie. and isn't this what i've always dreamed of? being some sort of magic? some sort of wicked? ~~love boys~~ I have neglected and disappointed me in relationships. i can be a good girlfriend or i can love myself. i can't do both at the same time. when i commit it is all, it is all or it is nothing. i won't have you with your foot already out the door. i will care for you deeply, unconditionally. this is not always a good thing. this has rarely ever been a good thing.

the therapy has been working (i swear).

but sometimes the sound of a notification can still send me spiralling, afraid it is him come back again to hurt me one more time. and once more. and once more. i turned my phone off for days, it became silent for years. you can take the girl out of the abusive relationship. but you can't take the abusive relationship out of the girl. somewhere inside we are all drowning in the water we were led to, sometimes we were the ones fetching it.

i'm accustomed to people leaving and there is a match under my bed with your name on it so that i'm ready to burn our bridge at any moment's notice. i'm sorry. my walls are high and i probably won't ever let you in. but if you're lucky. i might build you a small encampment. just outside it. and at night. if you look in just the right way. you can see there is a candle in the highest window that is burning just for you.

i won't tell you, but i'd like you to hold me. all of the time. seriously. all of the time. i want the forehead kisses. your hand on the small of my back. you holding me closely. so so closely. i can never get enough affection. i. can. never. get. enough. affection. i want to hear you say it, i want to hear how much you care, constantly. i want it all. i want healing like a pill i can crush into powder and stain my nostrils blue, sick with the wanting of it. i want you to be as hungry as i am to prove something. but while i'm proving love does not exist you are squeezing my hand saying *yes, yes it does*.

understand that love has been nothing but my undoing and i'm tired of stitching myself back together. i can't keep putting myself back together like this. i am tired of healing. i am tired of getting over someone. from day one i will be preparing for the day you leave.
i'm sorry.

i am anxiety poured into a human mould and it never set quite right. sometimes I forget the world won't come crashing down on me if i take a moment to breathe. sometimes means all the time. i have been apologising

for the inconvenience of my existence for so long. i have
been writing this sad poetry for so long. i want you to
give me a reason to write one of love. one where i
compare your smile to sunlight on a winter morning
and etch out the exact frequency my heart beats when
you kiss me.

i want you to read this poem. i want you to peel back
every dark desperate part of me. would it be easier
if you were my enemy first and then my lover? if i
give you enough warning does it mean you will stay when
the trauma starts spilling out? when i stop being a pixie
and start being a real girl?

understand that this doesn't have to be forever. but if
you do leave. please do so gently. i'll grit my teeth.
i'll move on. i've done it before. i've done it before.

i'm scared. i'm so fucking scared. but i've decided to
give you my heart and i hope you understand what a
rare and beautiful gift you've been given.
be kind to it. please.

Over a Year Gone

Time has lulled me on the passage of fading memory

far more than I'd like to admit –

It's funny,

the feelings around you have gone soft again.

Gelatinous teeth, dissolving into something sticky.

The silence is sweet.

I do not seethe with the sharpness of anger.

I do not drown in the heaviness of despair.

Time has, in fact, pulled the edges inward.

Not so much moving on, as simply just going on with my life.

When there are new wounds to tend to,

the itch of this scar doesn't demand so loudly.

The memories are salt in the ocean.

I know it's there, but I cannot see it.

I can go plunging into it if I want,

an open cut can taste the sting

If I want.

But I lie belly up instead, I float in the density of it all.

The sun is so warm.

Acknowledgments

Thank you to the beautiful people who saw me through the hardest part of my life, your unwavering kindness, love, and gentleness saved me.

To my mum who was there every time I cried, who held me and validated my reality. Who showed me what was right and what was wrong. To my dad who was a calm and steady presence, who made me realise just how wrong his actions were. To my brothers who saw me in all my rage and sadness, who would come with candy or a quip to cheer me up.

To Poojaa Balasubramanian who was always there for me, no matter how much I talked about the same thing over and over again. Your unending wisdom and patience mean more than I could ever tell you.

To Kate Thompson who understood me better than I sometimes understand myself, you helped me remember all the years that came before him, and all the years that will come after him.

To Alannah Tennant, for all the walks, and making me laugh even when all I wanted to do was cry. For showing me how to be strong when I felt weak, for being angry for me when all I felt was numbness.

To Vaani Guruparan who made me feel light even on my heaviest days, for listening without judgment and distracting me from my pain.

To Leddra Grierson who lets me know when I'm overthinking, for listening to my poetry, even when it wasn't very good.

To all the friends I couldn't list here, to the strangers who heard my story, to the strangers who have shared their own stories.

To Jacob, the one who came next, who showed me what real healthy love is.

A Note About the Author

A girl with too many emotions and too small of a body to contain them all, Doné de Beer writes to ease the pain of this sticky life. Whenever anything bad happens in her life, her response is always 'well, at least this will make for a good poem'.

She writes for the too-sensitive people, the emotional ones, the bleeding hearts. She wants to soothe them, hold them, call them out, push them, to be the itch of the healing.

This is the first book she has ever self-published, and she hopes you will be gentle with her about it.

You can find her on Tik Tok and Instagram @donewithwriting or go to her website donedebeer.com.

If you resonated with any part of this book, please know you're not alone. For confidential support with domestic abuse please contact 1800RESPECT at 1800 737 732.

www.ingramcontent.com/pod-product-compliance
Lightning Source LLC
Chambersburg PA
CBHW071252070526
44583CB00017B/2440